THE GREAT BOOK OF

RACING CARS

THE GREAT BOOK OF

RACING CARS

Text by Paul Harmer

Rourke Enterprises, Inc.

Vero Beach, FL 32964

Library of Congress Cataloging-in-Publication Data

Harmer, Paul, 1960–
  The great book of racing cars.

  Includes index.
  Summary: Traces the history of automobile racing and describes the
evolution of some famous racing cars.
  1. Automobile racing—History—Juvenile literature.
2. Automobiles, Racing—History—Juvenile literature.
[1. Automobile racing—History 2. Automobiles, Racing—History]
I. Title.
GV1029.15.H36 1988   796.7′2′09   87-37632
ISBN 0-86592-455-4

Contents

Setting the Pace

Grand Prix: In motor racing terms, the words, *Grand Prix* bring to mind an image of fantastic speeds and noisy engines from a pack of bright colored racing cars tearing around a track.

The title is French and means big prize. Many of the world's big sporting events are known as Grand Prix. Motor racing's first Grand Prix was held in France over 80 years ago.

Then, ordinary streets and roads were closed to other traffic, such as it was in those early days of the motor vehicle. The racing cars that took part came in all shapes and sizes.

Much has changed. Just as the car, and the roads on which it is used, have improved, so motor racing has become far more organized. Great steps to ensure safety for all concerned have been taken.

Man has always looked for a challenge. A race against another. With the car came the chance to build a better car and to race one another. As word spread of new ideas to increase speed, or tires that gripped the road better, racing enthusiasts began to envision a worldwide competition to decide the global champion of car racing.

Grand Prix racing has become a huge industry employing many thousands of people worldwide.

It was not until after the Second World War that a Grand Prix motor racing championship was started. Previous Grand Prix races had been held in a number of countries, but in 1950 a championship was staged where points were awarded to the finishers:

1st: 8 pts	2nd: 6
3rd: 4	4th: 3
5th: 2.	

There was another point for the racing driver who set the fastest lap during the race.

At the end of the season the driver with the most points was the World Champion.

Seven races were held in that first year: England (Silverstone), France (Monaco and Rheims), USA (Indianapolis), Switzerland (Bremgarten), Belgium (Spa-Francorchamps) and Italy (Monza).

rollbar

rear wing

saudia

Mobil

saudia

TAG Tec d'

GOOD YEAR

wide slick tires

Ley

Sitting Comfortably

The cockpit of a Formula 1 racing car is just big enough for the driver. His seat is molded to his shape during the car's construction—a snug fit is essential. In front of him is a small steering wheel, which is detachable to make it easy to get in and out quickly. The gearshift is to the right, and current Grand Prix cars have a number of instruments on the panel. These tell the driver the turbo reading, gas consumption and oil pressure. Some cars even have a digital display for lap times, and most drivers are in radio contact with their pit crews.

Viewed from this angle, the tight fit of the driver, Nelson Piquet, is clearly visible (above) inside the cockpit of the 1986 Williams Formula I. Below: the cockpit, where the driver half sits and half lies, is right at the front of the car. The massive engine, radiator and fuel tanks take up the rest of the space.

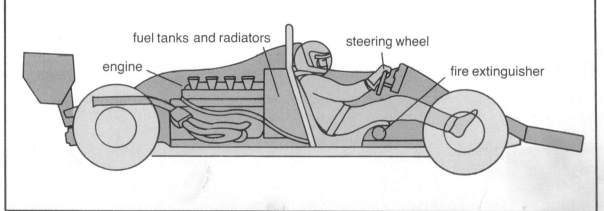

fuel tanks and radiators   steering wheel

engine   fire extinguisher

rearview mirror

The car below is Carlos Reutemann's Williams FW07C built for the 1981 Grand Prix season. The Argentine driver very nearly became World Champion; he came in second to Nelson Piquet.

smaller front wheels

front spoiler

Nearly a Century of Grand Prix Racing

Formula 1 is motor racing's top class. A series of Grand Prix races, usually 16, are held each year at selected circuits to count for the World Championship.

The first motor race to use the title Grand Prix was at Le Mans, in France, in 1906 but it was several years before the rules were fully set out. By the mid-1920s other European countries were holding their own Grand Prix races to a set of common Formula 1 regulations.

Those early cars used a maximum size engine of 13,000 cc (13-litre) and had to weigh around 1,750 lbs, and a mechanic had to ride alongside the driver The average speed achieved was between 70 and 100 miles per hour.

The Invaluable Mobile Mechanic

In the earliest days of the motor car it was not unusual for them to suffer mechanical breakdown, so the riding mechanic was an important passenger. He could adjust mixture control on the engine to give a better flow of gas, and on some cars it was the mechanic who operated the rear brakes. He would also keep a look out for other cars coming up behind.

The two-seater Mercedes racer of the 1914 era.

Following a number of crashes in which the mechanic was sometimes thrown out along with the driver, the mechanic stopped riding in the race in 1924.

Leather flying helmets and goggles were the only head protection worn. The seatbelt, if it was fitted at all, was a single lap-strap which could, depending on the accident, make matters worse—for no one had thought of roll-over bars then.

After the first decade of motor racing, cars were built with smaller engines, but the body of the car, the chassis, was altogether lighter than before. This enabled great speed to be achieved.

In 1927 the rules were revised to allow single-seater bodied cars, and this gave new opportunities. The major car makers of the time used their fast-improving road-going cars to try out ideas for making high-performance racing cars.

Brooklands (above), in Surrey, England was the world's first purpose built racing track. Until 1907 races had been held on public roads which were loosely marked off from other traffic and had little, if any, means of safety for spectators who simply lined the roads eager for the action. The $2\frac{3}{4}$ miles Brooklands track had steeply banked bends which enabled cars to travel much faster and provided spectacular viewing opportunities for spectators. Other "purpose-built" race tracks followed, but a famous so-called street circuit remains – the legendary Monaco – around the harbor streets of Monte Carlo and, more recently Dallas, Las Vegas and Detroit have laid out tracks around the city roads for Grand Prix racing.

The Indianapolis Speed Track

The Indianapolis 500 is America's most famous race and is renowned worldwide for the very high speeds attained around the $2\frac{1}{2}$ mile track. High banked curves, which are difficult to walk up, help increase the cornering speeds of the specially built 200 mph racing cars. The Indiana Speedway was built in 1909 as one of the world's first purpose built race tracks. But the early track surface broke up and the owners hit upon the idea of laying a brick foundation; some $3\frac{1}{4}$ million bricks were used and the track got the nickname of "The Brickyard".

The first "Indy 500" race was run in 1911 and attracted 40 entries and a massive crowd of 80,000 people. Winner of the first Indy 500, Ray Harroun, averaged 74.40 miles an hour to win the 500-mile race.

Ray Harroun in his Marmon Wasp. This was the first racing car to have a rear view mirror fitted: the "old" two-seater cars had all relied on the mechanic looking behind and warning the driver if anyone was close on his tail.

The officially recognized start date for World Championship Formula 1 was 1950, when a body known as FIA (Federation International de l'Automobile) selected six countries to run Grand Prix races and added the already famous Indianapolis 500 to count for the title.

The series started on May 13 at Silverstone, England. The 70-lap race was won by a 43-year-old Italian, Giuseppe Farina, in an Alfa Romeo Type 158. Races at Monaco, the Indy 500, Switzerland, Belgium, and France followed. The final round was at Monza, Italy: an ideal setting to crown motor racing's first World Champion, Farina.

By 1950 the cars were allowed a maximum of $2\frac{1}{2}$ liter engine or, if they were super-charged, 750 cc, and Ferrari, Alfa Romeo, and Maserati dominated. Juan Fangio, Stirling Moss, and Alberto Ascari were the drivers of that era—names that captured the imagination of the racing public.

Juan Fangio racing at Silverstone, England in an Alfa Romeo 158. Alfa Romeo and Ferrari cars dominated the tracks in the 1950s.

Juan Manuel Fangio was 40 years old when he won the first of his five Formula 1 Drivers World Championship titles in 1951. Although he had experience of being a riding mechanic in his home country of Argentina, Fangio did not take up racing himself until he was 37 years old. He was soon successful and was asked to drive by Alfa Romeo. In 1950 he finished runner-up to Farina, at the first ever World Championship. Although an accident at Monza, Italy in 1952 kept him away from the tracks, he stormed back to dominate the Grand Prix races with Maserati, Mercedes, and Ferrari. He won the World Championship for four successive years from 1954 to 1957. Fangio is still rated as one of the best Grand Prix drivers, and no other driver has yet won five World titles.

Three of the favorites line up for the start of the 1953 Grand Prix at Monza, Italy. Alberto Ascari is in the Ferrari no. 4. Giuseppe Farina is also in a Ferrari No. 6, and Juan Fangio is driving the Maserati No. 50.

Sponsorship means paying to have your name—like these above—seen by millions of people on the cars, worn by the drivers, and around the tracks. The Benetton team colors cannot be missed (below) under the imposing skyline of Detroit.

The World Championships grew in importance. Specialist race car makers emerged along with gearbox, engine, and tire producers, all improving their product with lessons learned from high speed competition. Ferrari and Lotus were soon challenged by Cooper, Brabham, Tyrrell, and McLaren. And as the cars improved, costs of remaining competitive increased. By the early seventies it was obvious that commercial sponsorship would give a financial boost to the image of Grand Prix racing. Major companies invested anything between $500,000 and $1,000,000 to have their names on the bodies of the cars. With the help of a worldwide television audience, motor racing's top attraction developed into very big business. New opportunities to increase the impact, such as special street circuits around Las Vegas, Dallas, and Detroit, were introduced, and countries such as Hungary and Mexico built new tracks to earn a place on the Grand Prix calendar in 1986.

The first World Champion was **Giuseppe Farina,** a doctor of political science. He was the eldest of three brothers whose Pininfarina factory became world famous for body styling—not just of racing, but road cars too.

Farina's arms stretched out, and his cool, relaxed driving style was copied by many other drivers. The 43-year-old Italian was an early hero. But little success followed. He had a series of crashes during a stay with the Ferrari team. He retired in 1955, but he did compete in the Indy 500 in 1956 and 1957. Although Farina had survived so many alarming race car crashes, he was to lose his life in a car accident when his car hit a telegraph pole on his way to watch the 1966 French Grand Prix.

Machines Need Men

Like many of the early racing drivers, **Graham Hill** worked as a mechanic for a team before getting his chance to drive cars for the then Lotus Team. Then he joined British Racing Motors (BRM) and won the World Championship in 1962. He rejoined Lotus and lifted the team's spirit when they had lost number 1 driver Jim Clark, and won the World Championship again in 1968. Hill retired and concentrated on running his own team. It was a tragedy that after 22 years of successful racing he then lost his life in a helicopter crash in England. His son Damon is currently racing well in British Formula 3.

Nigel Mansell is Britain's greatest driver since James Hunt, the 1976 World Champion. Mansell, like many drivers, gave up plenty of things that most people take for granted to concentrate on becoming a Formula 1 race driver. He suffered some dreadful accidents in Formula 3, a learning category, before making an impact with Lotus. But Mansell really arrived on the scene when he was given a chance by the Williams team. He was close runner-up in the 1986 World Championship and one of the fastest men of 1987, just beaten by Nelson Piquet, who gained the world title that year.

In the history of motor racing there have been many drivers whose fearless will and dashing speed earned them worldwide fame. The earliest of these drivers were Fangio and Moss, then Brabham, Hill, Stewart, Lauda, and most recently Prost, Brabham, Hill, Stewart, and Mario Andretti now have sons who are beginning to establish themselves. World Sportscar Champion Derek Bell's son Justin and David Hunt, the younger brother of 1976 World Champion James Hunt, are also set for future stardom.

The early World Champions did not make a fortune from motor racing, although it was rewarding. Many of them had other work to occupy them during the week, or worked for the teams that built the cars and some drivers even paid to race in a Grand Prix team.

These days, as well as being highly paid for racing, it is a full time job for Formula 1 drivers. Throughout the season, and even during the winter, they are kept busy with lots of testing. And now that sponsors play such a big part in the world of grand prix racing, every driver spends many days during the year making special appearances at shows and presentations to help promote his sponsor's products.

Far left: Graham Hill gazes upwards, goggles raised.
Left: Nigel Mansell wears the full-face helmet that is the style today.

Paul Stewart, above, is the elder son of three times World Champion Jackie Stewart and, below, is Gary Brabham, the middle son of Sir Jack Brabham—racing sons of racing fathers.

This picture of Nigel Mansell stepping into his Williams car clearly shows the full protective clothing that modern day Grand Prix drivers must wear. From head to foot they are covered in fire resistant overalls, and, as an extra safety measure, they have flame proof underwear too. Beneath the full face helmet a flame proof hood protects the head in the event of a fire. Tough straps form the safety harness and a roll bar adds protection in the event of an accident.

Learning the Way

In motor racing, speed along the straight part of the route is vital. The racing cars must reach their top speed as soon as possible after each corner. The corners are made to slow the cars down, but the drivers look for the fastest way, called the "line" or the "racing line."

The faster a car goes around a corner, the more speed it can build up along the next straight. To be slow out of a bend means that it will take longer for the car to reach its best speed. Even a fraction of a second can mean many lengths lost.

Racing drivers use a technique called "straight-lining a bend." They place the car on the outside of the track entering a bend and aim for the sharpest point of the corner, the "apex," which is used as a cutting point. The car then drifts wide finishing up on the outside of the track again.

If there is a series of tight bends, the driver decides which of these can be taken fastest; often a driver will enter the first part of a series of bends more slowly in order to get the right racing line for the next bend.

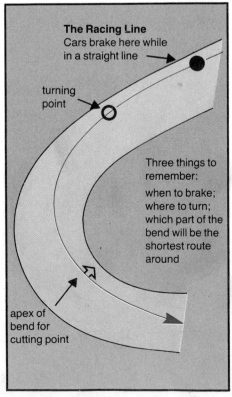

The Racing Line
Cars brake here while in a straight line

turning point

Three things to remember:

when to brake; where to turn; which part of the bend will be the shortest route around

apex of bend for cutting point

Training Program

How does a driver learn to race? People often talk of natural talent but even if a driver is quick it does not always make him a good racing driver. For most, it is a matter of practice makes perfect.

There are many types of racing: sedans, sports cars, single-seater racers. Not every driver wants to become a World Champion in Formula 1. Many race car drivers compete seriously, but for fun. But almost every one of them will have gone to a racing school, a kind of advanced driving school, to learn the finer points of race car driving.

The racing school teachers can point out where to brake for a corner: perhaps it is

At the world-famous Brands Hatch Circuit, in England (bottom), there is a Racing School where pupils graduate through sedans to single-seaters (below and below left) with expert instruction from professional racing drivers.

part of the track where the tarmac changes color slightly or near a banner by the trackside. Even in Grand Prix racing when drivers react instantly at great speeds, they know to within inches exactly where they must brake and slow down.

But even for the best pupils it is a struggle to get to the top in motor racing. Some schools offer prizes of a free race to the most promising. Young drivers usually invest all their money in racing and try to make a name for themselves, all in hopes of attracting a company sponsor to fund them.

Ferrari at the Forefront

Ferrari is one of the best known racing cars in the world. Yet Enzo Ferrari, the team owner, began his career with Alfa Romeo after World War I. His early successes came with sports cars in the Mille Miglia, a long distance race. The first Ferrari Formula 1 Grand Prix car did not appear until 1948 when Giuseppe Farina, Raymond Sommer, and B. Bira raced three Tipo 125s at Valentino in the Italian Grand Prix.

Although Ferrari's success in Grand Prix motor racing is legendary, Ferraris have suffered dreadful misfortune too. Wolfgang von Trips and many spectators were killed when the German driver crashed after a collision with Jim Clark. Gilles Villeneuve lost his life in a crash at Zolder in 1977. Ferrari remain as the only team to build everything for their racing cars "in-house" and, in terms of race victories, are the "winningest" team since Grand Prix racing began.

Ferrari's first major successes came with Fangio's driving of the Lancia modified car in 1956. Ferrari's next triumph was the famed Dino, one of the last front-engined Grand Prix cars, which was named after Enzo Ferrari's dying son. Mike Hawthorn of England (1958), Phil Hill of the United States (1961), and John Surtees of England (1964) took Dino versions to World Championship successes. Above: Wolfgang von Trips drives the Ferrari Dino at the 1958 Monaco Grand Prix.

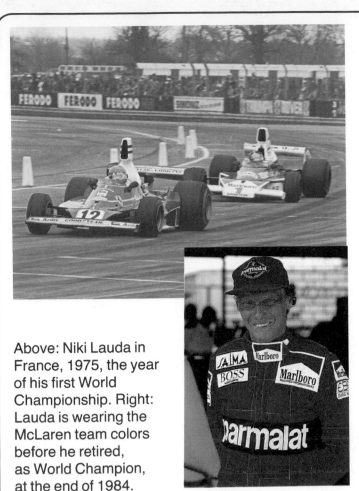

The Austrian **Niki Lauda** rates high as one of the all time greats, certainly in the modern era of motor racing. His driving skills attracted the big teams, who soon signed him up. He joined Ferrari in 1974.

The following year he was World Champion. But he had a terrible crash in 1976 at the Nurburgring in Germany and nearly died.

Miraculously, he recovered from dreadful burns, and six weeks later he returned to racing. Although many thought he was not fully fit, the brave Lauda wanted to hold onto his Champion's title. That year Britain's James Hunt beat him by 1 point.

Lauda had two poor years, by his standard, and quit in 1979. He came back to Grand Prix racing in 1982 with the McLaren team and in 1984 crowned an impressive career by winning the World title again.

Above: Niki Lauda in France, 1975, the year of his first World Championship. Right: Lauda is wearing the McLaren team colors before he retired, as World Champion, at the end of 1984.

It was ten years since the victories of the late fifties and early sixties before Ferrari got back into World Championship form. The new Ferrari 312T won the Constructor's Championship in 1975, 1976 and 1977, and again in 1979 when Jody Scheckter became the World Champion driver. His car, seen left, did not suffer a single mechanical breakdown that year.

Streamlined For Speed

Formula 1 racing cars, and indeed most single-seater racing cars, are built to exacting standards. The lighter a car is, the faster it will travel and through the years the rules have been changed to keep up with the latest inventions. Nowadays all Formula 1 cars have to weigh a minimum of 1,200 lbs, or if they are not turbo-powered, 1,000 lbs. All the cars are built around a "monocoque," a long, slim tub made of extremely strong but lightweight carbon-fiber material which has been developed from knowledge gained in the aircraft industry. The monocoque is designed to withstand considerable force in the event of a high-speed crash. The wheels and suspension are mounted in such a way that they help stabilize the car at speed. To assist further the car's stability, "aerofoils" are fitted to both ends of the car. The effect of these and the science of aerodynamics is described on the page opposite.

Lotus pit mechanics fly into action. The lightweight body, the monocoque, is clearly visible showing the strong tub, or cell, which protects the driver.

Current Formula 1 cars are designed to push through the air with the minimum resistance, the Ferrari (right) shows the influence of a slipstream body which uses the air passing over it to help force the car down at high speeds.

Aerodynamics

The faster the racing car goes (right) the more violent the air becomes beneath it. It forces the body upwards, the tires produce less grip and power is lost.

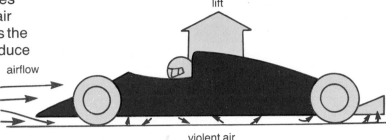

lift

airflow

violent air

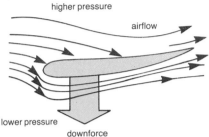

higher pressure

airflow

lower pressure

downforce

Aerofoils are used on single-seater racing cars, like upside-down aircraft wings (left). They are attached front and rear to the cars to use the airflow for downforce.

The air beneath the aerofoil is made to go further and faster than the air above, this uses the higher pressure above the aerofoil to force the car down at high speeds.

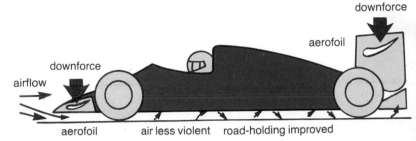

downforce

aerofoil

downforce

airflow

aerofoil

air less violent   road-holding improved

Lotus

Jim Clark was a quiet person, almost shy, but he had enormous talent as a racing driver and won 25 Grand Prix races in a tragically short career. The Scottish-born Clark joined Team Lotus in 1960 and gradually became their number one driver. The Lotus 25 and Jimmy Clark were a true force; only mechanical trouble in the last race stopped Clark from becoming the 1962 World Champion. But nothing could stop him the next time; he sped to seven victories—a record number in one year—to become World Champion. The mechanical problems returned in 1964, but again Clark fought back the next year. He reclaimed the driver's crown and also won the Indy 500. The Lotus 49 developed mechanical trouble again in 1967, and despite four GP victories Clark's title chances faded. In 1968 while taking part in a Formula 2 race at Hockenheim, Clark crashed at high speed and lost his life.

The Lotus 25 (top, and above driven by Jim Clark) was the first "monocoque" racing car. The body, or monocoque, is made up of a strong, lightweight shell.

Like Ferrari, Lotus ranks as a world-famous name in Grand Prix motor racing. The company's success owes much to the ingenious flair of its founder Colin Chapman, who continually surprised his rival race car designers with new trends.

Chapman designed the Lotus 25 and the Lotus 49, in which Jim Clark drove to success. Then in 1978 Lotus introduced the first "ground effect" car, the 79, which used the airflow to suck the car to the track and produce increased speeds and better cornering ability.

Despite such acclaim the Lotus history has been tinged with tragedy: Jim Clark died in 1968, Jochen Rindt was killed in practice at Monza in 1970 and was the first posthumous World Champion, and Ronnie Peterson's crash at Monza in 1979 also proved fatal.

Ronnie Peterson (right) was regarded as one of the fastest Grand Prix drivers in the early seventies. The Swede joined Lotus in 1973 as teammate to Emerson Fittipaldi and won seven races. Peterson and Mario Andretti teamed up in the hugely successful Lotus 78 and 79 cars and were virtually unbeatable.

Bottom: Nearly ten years later the young Ayrton Senna drives for Lotus in the 1987 Brazilian Grand Prix.

Mario Andretti was born in Italy. He was 12 when he watched Ascari winning at Monza in 1952 and decided he wanted to be a race driver. Still a teenager, his family moved to America and Andretti began racing on the dirt tracks and ovals before graduating to the USAC Series. Andretti is best known for his success on the oval racetracks. He was USAC Champion in 1965, 1966, and 1969, and also won the 1969 Indy 500.

Andretti's first Formula 1 Grand Prix was with Team Lotus in 1968. In 1977 he finished third in the World Championship. The next year the dominant Lotus 79 ground effect design won him the World F1 Championship.

Along with one of his sons, Michael, he is back racing Indy cars these days.

Engine Power

The development of the Ford Cosworth DFV engine and the stunning success that followed is a major landmark in the history of Grand Prix racing. Keith Duckworth and Frank Costin, together with Colin Chapman of Lotus and senior technicians at Ford, combined their talents to produce the 3-liter engine for Grand Prix racing. The first engine was used to power the Lotuses of Jim Clark and Graham Hill. The car did not just win but totally overpowered all the opposition in the 1967 Dutch Grand Prix at Zandvoort. Soon every team except Ferrari, who built their own engines, were equipped with the robust V8s. These mass-produced engines claimed no fewer than 155 Grand Prix victories up until 1983, when the turbo engine was introduced.

Jim Clark sits on the Zandvoort grid in 1967, anxious to give the 8-cylinder Cosworth engine a debut victory in his Lotus 49.

The Turbo

The power of an engine depends on just how quickly the fuel and air can be mixed and pushed into the cylinders. Most cars get their fuel from something called a carburetor. The engine draws in air, and with it gasoline, through this device.

The system of fuel injection forces measured amounts of gasoline into the engine so that the best balance of fuel and air are in the engine together.

The turbocharger was developed to force still more fuel and air into the engine under pressure. It is designed to use wasted gases from the exhaust as energy to turn a small turbine. The turbine drives a special compressor, an impeller. The impeller pressurizes the air at the point where fuel is injected.

To do this efficiently and produce something like 30 percent more power—the turbocharger revolves at an incredibly high speed and gets very hot. An inter-cooler working on the same system as a car's radiator cools the engine.

Turbocharging made a big impact in Grand Prix racing as early as 1983 and boosted the top speeds of the cars to more than 200 M.P.H. These high speeds created a risk, and many racetracks around the world could not keep up with the need for extra safety modifications. In 1989 the Formula 1 cars will no longer use turbo engines but will be restricted to "normally aspirated," engines. But the success of turbocharging in Grand Prix racing has benefited the design of everyday cars.

Above: the twin turbochargers on this Porsche TAG turbo engine can be seen on either side of the engine connected to the exhaust system. Below: the two bladed wheels of the turbocharger are mounted on a common pin. The wheel on the left, the turbine, is located in the exhaust gas path (shown in red). When the driver presses the accelerator pedal, the speed with which the exhaust gases flow out of the engine increases. The turbine goes around faster. This causes the wheel on the right, the impeller, to spin. The impeller is set in the air inlet to the engine. The faster the impeller goes, the faster air from outside (shown in blue) is sucked in and pushed along the inlet pipes where the fuel passes through to the engine. The faster the engine runs the faster the exhaust gases spin the turbine and the quicker the impeller rotates. More and more air and fuel is forced into the engine.

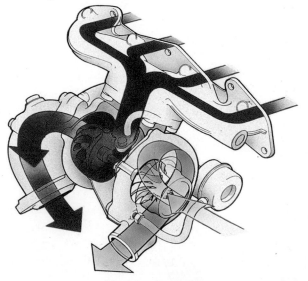

Tyrrell Fights Back

Ken Tyrrell, owner of the Tyrrell Racing Team, has an unusual background. Prior to being a successful Grand Prix car designer, he ran a large timber business in Surrey, England. Tyrrell is known for discovering and encouraging new talent, and John Surtees, Jackie Stewart, Jacky Ickx, and Martin Brundle are some of the drivers to have benefited from his care. Sixteen of Jackie Stewart's 27 Grand Prix victories were achieved in cars designed by Tyrrell.

Right: the Tyrrell 006, another World Championship winning car for Stewart in 1973.

The World Champion of 1969, 1971, and 1973, and runner-up in 1972, **Jackie Stewart** brought a business-like expertise to motor racing. Born on June 11, 1943, Stewart was the son of a garage owner. He soon got to know his cars, but his parents did not want him to race and his career did not start until he was 21 years old. Until then his first love had been clay pigeon shooting, a sport in which his smooth, concentrated style saw him rise to the top. He joined Ken Tyrrell to race Formula 3 Coopers in 1964. He was soon entrusted with Formula 2 cars and had begun to attract the attention of the biggest racing teams. Stewart's first Grand Prix win was in Italy for BRM in 1965, but when Tyrrell at last formed a Formula 1 team, Stewart returned to take the first of his World titles in the speedy Matra. In 1973 Stewart retired from Grand prix motor racing after the death of his friend and teammate Francois Cevert. His brilliant career netted 27 Grand Prix victories, and it is rumored that in 1979 he was offered almost $5 million to make a comeback. The Scot turned it down, and these days he enjoys a safer life commentating, but is still much involved with car racing.

Left: Jackie Stewart en route to victory at Monaco in 1971. He won six races that year for Tyrrell.

The present Tyrrell challenger is unique because it has been completely designed by computer, using information from Data General, one of the team's sponsors.

This latest DG016 car is powered by a non turbo Ford Cosworth DFY engine. Tyrrell planned ahead for when the Turbo engine is no longer used in Formula 1. The special carbon-fiber bodywork, very light but extremely strong, is made by Courtaulds, another of the team sponsors. In 1987 Britain's Jonathan Palmer and Frenchman Philippe Streiff were leading drivers in the non-turbo class in Grand Prix racing. Palmer won the 1987 Jim Clark Cup as champion of the class.

Below: up-to-date Tyrrell: French driver Philippe Streiff in the Tyrrell-Ford at Monaco in 1987.

In Search of Speed

Grand Prix racing has always been a testing ground for technical invention. The Tyrrell team built a six wheeler car. Jack Brabham tried to improve the aerodynamics of his car by means of two wings set high up on stilts.

Once again, though, it was Colin Chapman, a most brilliant designer, whose technical experimentation was to have lasting success. Chapman's masterpiece was the concept of ground effect, which sucked the cars to the track at high speed, making them faster and smoother.

Team Tyrrell astounded their Grand Prix rivals with the Tyrrell P34 six-wheeler in 1976. The four wheels at the front had less width than the normal four wheeled cars. It was hoped that they would therefore improve aerodynamics and give twice as much grip. The

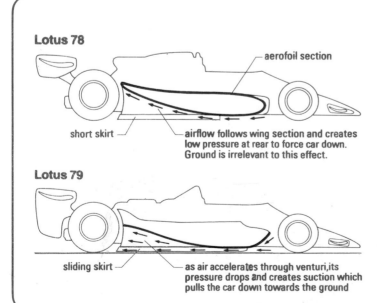

Lotus 78

aerofoil section

short skirt

airflow follows wing section and creates low pressure at rear to force car down. Ground is irrelevant to this effect.

Lotus 79

sliding skirt

as air accelerates through venturi, its pressure drops and creates suction which pulls the car down towards the ground

Ground Effect Explained

Racing cars have always been designed to make the best use of the air through which they travel. For instance, the upper bodywork of the car is designed so that the air passing over it helps force the car down onto the road. In the seventies, designers experimented with the shapes underneath the cars. Suction was produced by air passing through the narrow gap between the track and the specially made side-pods of the car. This gap formed a "wind tunnel" or "venturi". The suction helped keep

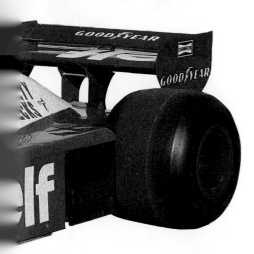

Flying High

Jack Brabham was the first and only driver ever to win a World Championship in a car of his own design. Brabham had teamed up with his friend Ron Tauranac to design and build the Brabhams using Repco engines. In the 1960s the use of wings as a means of cheating the wind had not been fully developed. It was very much copying another team's idea, and some teams had not even fitted such devices to their cars yet. For the 1968 season Brabham's BT26 car appeared with two wings at the rear, set high up on stilts. When one of these wings buckled under stress, officials decided they should be banned in case they came off completely and caused danger.

team was encouraged when Jody Scheckter claimed pole position and won the Swedish Grand Prix, but their success was not to last. The cars suffered from too much tire wear. Ronnie Peterson and Patrick Depailler struggled on when Scheckter left the team disillusioned, but the P34 was shelved. The designer, Derek Gardner, left the team and was replaced by former Lotus man Maurice Phillippe, who built the 008 in time for 1977.

the car low on the track at high speed. This became known as Ground effect.

Ronnie Peterson's Lotus 79 shows clearly the sliding skirt that cuts out the air between car and track. Note also the wide "pods" used to carry the skirts.

Brabham : Australian Inheritance

With many successes to his credit in Australia, Jack Brabham came to England in 1955 to further his racing career. He drove for the Cooper Team and was able to combine his mechanical knowledge with his talent as a driver to win the 1959 and 1960 World Championships. He invited Ron Tauranac, a past rival from his early racing days, to come to England and help build a new car. Brabham did not want the cars to carry his name, and originally they were called MRD. The initials stood for Motor Racing Developments, their official company name. Brabham and Tauranac learned much by building cars for customers in the Formula 2, Formula 3, and Formula Junior categories. Jack Brabham finally changed his mind about the name of the cars. In 1966 at the age of 40 he returned to the Grand Prix scene to win the World Championship. It was the first and only time that a driver has won the title in a car he built himself.

By 1970 Jack Brabham had ended his partnership with Tauranac to enjoy retirement. Four years later Tauranac sold the business to Bernie Ecclestone, the current principal owner of the Brabham Racing Team.

Jack Brabham is seen in action in the Belgium Grand Prix in 1967. His third World title, in 1966, was at the wheel of his own car. This was the only time that a builder has driven a car of his own design to the World Championship.

Brazilian Nelson Piquet (above) stepped straight from Formula 3 into Grand Prix racing with the Brabham team. His first Grand Prix win was at Long Beach in 1980. Piquet spent seven years with the Brabham team and (below) he is seen, in 1983, during the Brazilian round, on his way to his second World Championship title for Brabham. The first was in 1981. Piquet signed with Williams in 1985 and won the World Championship in 1987. In 1988 he has replaced his fellow countryman Ayrton Senna at Lotus.

Jack Brabham's earliest races were for the Cooper team. Above he is seen at the Indianapolis 500.

Early Lessons

John Cooper was renowned in the 1950s and 1960s for his successful Formula 1, Formula 3, and Formula Junior cars. It was the Rob Walker team Cooper cars that helped launch the careers of Stirling Moss, Jack Brabham, and Bruce McLaren. Like Colin Chapman of Lotus, Cooper's genius often caught the opposition napping. His T51 Cooper-Climax was the first winning rear-engined Formula 1 car. His rivals told him it would not work, but it was good enough for Jack Brabham.

World Champion McLaren

Above: the McLaren M23 revealed. This is James Hunt's car. In 1976 Hunt won the World Championship in the M23. Alain Prost (right) and the McLaren TAG V6 have built up a strong partnership. The Frenchman won the World Championship in 1985 and 1986 and has now bettered Jackie Stewart's record.

Following a mixed early career in Formula 3, the dashing and somewhat outspoken **James Hunt** secured a rich English lord to back his bid for Formula 1 glory. His activities on and off the racetracks created newspaper headlines, but it was not until 1976 when he was signed up by McLaren that he really had a chance to show his skill. The battle for the World title was between Hunt in the Marlboro McLaren and Niki Lauda's Ferrari. Hunt's eight pole positions and eventual six Grand Prix wins earned him the title by one point. During the season, though, his Austrian rival had missed several races while recovering from a crash in West Germany. The following two years were not so good for the controversial Hunt. He was brave enough to admit, upon his retirement in 1979, that the Formula 1 cars were now going too fast for his taste.

Bruce McLaren's breakthrough as a race car designer came with the major successes of his big sports cars in the Canadian American Challenge (CanAm). While testing one of these cars in 1970 at Goodwood in

England, McLaren died. To continue McLaren's efforts, Teddy Mayer and fellow countryman Phil Kerr became joint principals of the team.

In the mid-seventies, before Lotus introduced the ground-effect design, McLaren enjoyed great success in Grand Prix racing with the M23. Emerson Fittipaldi (1975) and James Hunt (1976) won two consecutive World Championships in this car.

Recently the McLaren Team has won two consecutive World titles (1985 and 1986) with its MP4/2 which uses a TAG V6 Turbo engine, designed and built by Porsche.

Although France was where Grand Prix racing began, there had not been a French World Champion until **Alain Prost** secured the title in 1985. Prost's small but strong stature is ideal for the current Formula 1 racing cars. He was successful in Karts and Renault powered single-seaters before turning just as successfully to Formula 3 in 1979. But he did not make his Formula 1 debut until 1980, when he drove for McLaren. Soon afterward he joined Renault and won his first GP, in France in 1981. Prost returned to McLaren for the 1984 season and partnered Niki Lauda. Prost won seven of the races but still finished runner-up in the Championship. Since then Prost has continued the successful McLaren-TAG Porsche turbo link by winning the Championship in 1985 and 1986.

The Marlboro McLaren MP4/3

The Marlboro McLaren MP4 series have been the most successful cars of recent Grand Prix history.

The designers and builders make changes to their cars every year to keep ahead of their competitors on the circuits and to conform to the revisions that are always taking place within the rules of Grand Prix Formula I.

The McLaren MP4/3 demonstrates these subtle changes—for instance, in the styling of the body. The MP4/3 is also the first to feature a special valve that limits the effect of the turbocharge boost. Regulations are in force to reduce turbocharging and eventually ban it altogether.

ENGINE TAG (*Techniques d'Avant Garde*) developed by Porsche, 1500 cc Turbo
FUEL/OIL Shell
FUEL TANK 195 liters
TRANSMISSION 6-speed
CHASSIS Molded carbon-fiber/honeycomb composite
WHEELS Front 12″ (305 mm) **Rear** 16.5″ (419 mm)
TIRES Goodyear

Below: the Marlboro McLaren MP4/3 revealed. Bottom: the same car showing the body complete—now more angular than the previous MP4/2. The monocoques, or body shells, are all made at McLaren's factory in Woking, England. Until 1985 the body was made by the Hercules Corporation in North America. This specialist manufacturer played an important part in McLaren's search for success.

The Grand Prix Circuits

For reasons of safety and because today's Grand Prix cars go so much faster, many of the early tracks are no longer in use. The Monaco "street-circuit" is still in use. In Monaco, the average speed for a lap is only 87 miles per hour compared to Silverstone in England, one of the fastest GP tracks, where the average speed is 145 miles per hour.

The main circuits that have been in regular use in the 16 rounds of the World Grand Prix are:

Osterreichring, Austria		3.69 miles
Zolder, Belgium		2.64 miles
Spa, Belgium		4.31 miles
Rio, Brazil		3.12 miles
Paul Ricard, France		3.61 miles
Hockenheim, West Germany		4.21 miles
Brands Hatch, England		2.61 miles
Silverstone, England		2.96 miles
Monza, Italy		3.60 miles
Imola, Italy		3.13 miles
Monaco, Monte Carlo		2.08 miles
Estoril, Portugal		2.70 miles

Silverstone, 2.96 miles, (below) is one of the oldest and the fastest tracks in use by the Grand Prix teams. A new bend, just before the start line, has been added. On the straights the cars reach up to 210 miles per hour! 65 laps of this circuit are made each Grand Prix.

The newest circuits to be included in the Grand Prix are:

Adelaide, Australia	2.38 miles
***Gilles Villeneuve**, Canada	2.74 miles
Detroit, USA	2.56 miles
Budapest, Hungary	2.49 miles
Jerez, Spain	2.62 miles

*Canada circuit at Montreal named after Gilles Villeneuve, the French Canadian who tragically died at the wheel of his Ferrari.

The tricky street circuit of Monaco on the famous Riviera (right) offers very little opportunity for overtaking and mistakes can prove costly as there are hardly any run-off areas. The Italians are famous for their huge and loud support of everything to do with car racing, especially when it is one of their beloved red Ferraris. The San Marino circuit at Imola (below) and the famous Monza track each hold a Grand Prix during the season.

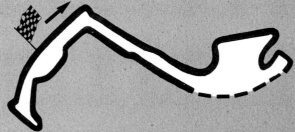

Monaco, 2.08 miles (above) winds through the Monte Carlo streets and even through a tunnel by the dockside. The drivers follow this route around 78 times during the Grand Prix. Imola (below) has recently been introduced so that Italy now has two Grand Prix races each year. Here, 60 laps of the 3.13 mile circuit are run each race.

Williams: Winning Formula

The Williams team suffered mixed fortunes and trailed just behind the best until the 1980s. Then the FW07B, designed by Patrick Head and a revision of the promising FW06, took Australian Alan Jones to 7 race wins and the 1980 World Championship. The present Williams FW11 uses a Honda V6 turbo engine. Drivers Nigel Mansell and Nelson Piquet are two of the quickest of the current race car drivers. Today Williams and their great rivals, the McLaren Team, share top status in Grand Prix racing.

In the 1986 World Championships Mansell scored five wins and Piquet four, out of the 16 races. Although this secured the Constructors title for Williams, Mansell's hopes of the driver's crown evaporated when he had a tire failure in the last round at Adelaide, Australia.

Left: Nigel Mansell celebrates in style after the 1987 French Grand Prix.

The great Australian driver Alan Jones helped make Williams a winning team. But the team's efforts in the 1978 season were overshadowed by the unbeatable "ground-effect" Lotuses. Equipped with the FW07 chassis the next year, Williams was well in the running. Jones had poor luck at the beginning of the year and it was his teammate Clay Regazzoni who secured the first Grand Prix win for a Williams car at Silverstone. Jones picked up four wins and just missed out on the title. But in 1980, with five wins, the title was his.

Keke Rosberg, (right) and in typical style at Monaco in his Williams (above), was a remarkable World Champion of 1982. The spectacular Finnish driver won only one Grand Prix, at Dijon-Prenois in Switzerland, but consistent placings earned him the title. Rosberg had raced for a number of teams without success. When Alan Jones announced he was leaving Williams, Rosberg boldly contacted Frank Williams, the Williams chief, asking to drive for them! Up until his retirement in 1986, Rosberg proved his title was no fluke. He had several more wins and earned a high rating as a top class Formula 1 driver.

Bottom: Nelson Piquet powers through the Brazilian countryside during the 1987 championship.

The Champions

In the race for ever-improving technology, Grand Prix Formula 1 racing has always stood as the top level in terms of motor sport achievement.

Below: the rules of Grand Prix racing have changed consistently but the Champion drivers remain.

World Champion Drivers		
1950	**Giuseppe Farina** Italy	Alfa Romeo
1951	**Juan Fangio** Argentina	Alfa Romeo
1952	**Alberto Ascari** Italy	Ferrari
1953	**Alberto Ascari** Italy	Ferrari
1954	**Juan Fangio** Argentina	Maserati & Mercedes-Benz
1955	**Juan Fangio** Argentina	Mercedes-Benz
1956	**Juan Fangio** Argentina	Ferrari
1957	**Juan Fangio** Argentina	Maserati
1958	**Mike Hawthorn** England	Ferrari
1959	**Jack Brabham** Australia	Cooper-Climax
1960	**Jack Brabham** Australia	Cooper-Climax
1961	**Phil Hill** USA	Ferrari
1962	**Graham Hill** England	BRM
1963	**Jim Clark** Scotland	Lotus-Climax
1964	**John Surtees** England	Ferrari
1965	**Jim Clark** Scotland	Lotus-Climax
1966	**Jack Brabham** Australia	Brabham Repco
1967	**Denis Hulme** New Zealand	Brabham Repco
1968	**Graham Hill** England	Lotus-Ford

World Champion Drivers		
1969	**Jackie Stewart** Scotland	Matra-Ford
1970	**Jochen Rindt** Austria	Lotus-Ford
1971	**Jackie Stewart** Scotland	Tyrrell-Ford
1972	**Emerson Fittipaldi** Brazil	Lotus-Ford
1973	**Jackie Stewart** Scotland	Tyrrell-Ford
1974	**Emerson Fittipaldi** Brazil	Lotus-Ford
1975	**Niki Lauda** Austria	Ferrari
1976	**James Hunt** England	McLaren
1977	**Niki Lauda** Austria	Ferrari
1978	**Mario Andretti** USA	Lotus
1979	**Jody Scheckter** South Africa	Ferrari
1980	**Alan Jones** Australia	Williams
1981	**Nelson Piquet** Brazil	Brabham
1982	**Keke Rosberg** Finland	Williams
1983	**Nelson Piquet** Brazil	Brabham
1984	**Niki Lauda** Austria	McLaren
1985	**Alain Prost** France	McLaren
1986	**Alain Prost** France	McLaren
1987	**Nelson Piquet** Brazil	Williams

The Constructors' World Championship

The Formula I car manufacturers also present their own award. Based on a system of points awarded to the cars, rather than the drivers, the big teams battle for this title too.

1958 Vanwall	1973 Lotus
1959 Cooper	1974 McLaren
1960 Cooper	1975 Ferrari
1961 Ferrari	1976 Ferrari
1962 Lotus	1977 Ferrari
1963 Lotus	1978 Lotus
1964 Ferrari	1979 Ferrari
1965 Lotus	1980 Williams
1966 Brabham	1981 Williams
1967 Brabham	1982 Ferrari
1968 Lotus	1983 Ferrari
1969 Matra	1984 McLaren
1970 Lotus	1985 McLaren
1971 Tyrrell	1986 Williams
1972 Lotus	1987 Williams

Three times World Champion Jackie Stewart (above left) set a record number of 27 wins, from 99 races, in his career. The talented Scottish-born driver brought a new meaning to the word professionalism in the sport. As well as being aware of the financial rewards that racing offered, he is responsible for vastly improving safety standards. The 1985 and 1986 World Champion Alain Prost (above right) was the first Frenchman to win the title and has bettered Stewart's record number of wins.

Stirling Moss, without a doubt the greatest Grand Prix driver *never* to have won the World title, remains as a true hero of the sport. His name is better known than many of the current drivers and he retired in 1962. With a tire ready to blow, he drove his Cooper-Climax to victory in the 1958 Argentine Grand Prix. This was the first Grand Prix win for a rear engine car. He won 16 of the 66 Grand Prix races he entered but had to settle for being runner-up to the title in 1955, 1956, 1957, and 1958, and third in 1959 and 1961.

Stirling Moss driving a Lotus in the 1961 Dutch Grand Prix, in which he finished 4th.

A Day at the Track

Flag Signals

Brightly colored flags are used by track officials, known as marshals, at various points around the circuit:

Blue Another car is close behind.

Red/yellow stripes Beware; the track ahead is slippery.

Yellow Great danger ahead; be prepared to slow down.

White A slow car is on the track ahead.

Green This usually appears at a point on the circuit after a yellow flag has been shown. It means that this part of the track is now clear.

Red The race has been stopped prematurely.

Black Can be used at various points around the circuit to signify the race has been halted.

Black/white chequered This is shown to the winner of the race.

There are two full days of testing and qualifying before each Grand Prix race. During that time the teams set the cars up to suit whichever circuit they are on. They can adjust the gear ratios to increase acceleration or maybe put in a special cog that will enable the driver to remain in a particular gear for a series of corners rather than have to shift up or down.

Each day has two sessions. The first is an untimed period when most of the setting up is done and the drivers have a practice period. Then there is an officially timed qualifying session when the cars have been tuned up and the drivers squeeze every mile per hour they can to be the fastest and gain pole position, the most favored place of all from which to start a race.

Overnight the technicians check the feedback from the driver and their own printouts from on-board computers, which measure every movement of the car. They might make adjustments to the car or try something new for the next session. In the end, though, they rely on the driver to achieve the target.

Above: cars line up on the starting grid at Brands Hatch, England, for the 1986 Grand Prix. The Williams team drivers, Piquet and Mansell, took pole and second grid positions respectively.

Race days are always accompanied by a host of sideshows, off-circuit activities, and supporting events in a bid to keep the huge crowd highly entertained from very early in the morning to late night. Most spectators will have arrived at the crack of dawn. Others camp there for the entire three days to enjoy the colorful scene.

The morning of the race, the Grand Prix cars have a final warm-up session and then take their grid places—fastest cars at the front, followed by the next fastest and so on—half an hour before the start of the race. With two minutes to go they complete a warm-up lap, the last chance to get heat into the tires to make sure that they work from the very start. Then they assemble back on the grid and await the red light (under starter's orders) and three to six seconds later the green: then they are off!

Pole Position

The driver who has been timed as the fastest in practice for the race starts in pole position. When races were started with flags, it meant the quickest driver started next to the man with the flag-pole.

The drivers with the most pole positions in Grand Prix races up to the end of 1986 are:

Jim Clark	33
Juan Manuel Fangio	28
Niki Lauda	24
Nelson Piquet	20
Mario Andretti	18
Rene Arnoux	18
Jackie Stewart	17
Stirling Moss	16
Alain Prost	16
Alberto Ascari	14
James Hunt	14
Ronnie Peterson	14

Team Spirit

The team mechanics' jobs are not over once the race starts. Far from it, since many things can happen during a race that need urgent attention. Then the driver will pull into the pits and rejoin the race as soon as he can. The most common pitstop is for new tires, and it is vital that the crew is ready—one to each wheel —to carry out this task in as short a time as possible. Sometimes it can take as little as 8 seconds to change all four!

Left: the Williams team, in their blue and yellow overalls, work to change the tires on Nigel Mansell's car. Above: the treaded tires show as Mansell drives on a wet track.

Below: pitcrews still rely on the "old fashioned" signal board to tell drivers what is happening, even after the introduction of driver-to-pit radios. The board can be used to tell the driver his current position, how many laps to go, and how many seconds he is behind the driver in front of him. They will often say "IN" meaning pull into the pits for tires, or can tell the driver if his rival has dropped out of the race.

Tires for all Weather

If the track is wet the cars run on treaded tires. The grooves provide an escape route for the water so the treaded part can grip the track.

If the track is dry, the treadless (slick) tire is made to grip the track and performs best when warm.

Timing

Modern day Grand Prix racing is precision timed by a computer system developed by Olivetti and Longines. The computer's record is transmitted to screen displays from which all drivers and team officials can see the times for every lap that each car does during practices and the race itself. This system is considerably more accurate than the hand held stop watches of yesteryear!

Olivetti and Longines are the official timekeepers for all Formula 1 Grand Prix races and travel to every race with as much back up and staff as a team itself. The cars break a timing beam on the start/finish line each time they pass through and all the information is recorded by a series of computers. At the very moment a car completes a lap, the time is beamed onto hundreds of screens for the teams, commentators and press to see. This information can be transmitted over live television to accompany the action. Often a driver who sets a time for the grid and then sees it beaten by another driver on the screen will come out again and go even faster, moving up the starting grid.

Above left: computer technology provides instant information to drivers and officials. Left: radio and clipboard are also indispensable tools for the back-up team. The driver keeps in touch with the pit through a radio link in his helmet.

The Back-Up Business

Above: the Camel Lotus Honda team gather round the car. Drivers, Ayrton Senna and Satoru Nakajima, would be nowhere without the support and efficiency of their back up team.

A huge number of people are involved in the day-to-day running of a Formula 1 Grand Prix team. Among these are the secretary who must make all the arrangements to get the cars and equipment to the racetracks throughout the world and the driver who looks after the trucks that carry the racing cars. When you see the driver alone on the grid waiting for the green light, it is easy to forget how many people are involved behind the scenes.

Long gone are the days when a driver and one or two mechanics loaded their car and spares on a trailer and set off each weekend.

Now every team is a major business and employs around 100 persons, each with a vital job. Up to 10 engineers are responsible for each car, and most teams have at least two cars ready for every race. As well as spare engines and gearboxes, other materials are needed: enough to completely rebuild the car if necessary.

At the trackside, computer timing is used and every team has a bank of timing screens that relay important information about the car.

To help pay for all this, the teams are sponsored by large companies who put their names on the race clothing of personnel and on the cars. In return, they get advertising coverage throughout the world for their products.

Glossary

Aerodynamic   A car's body is shaped so that it will ease the resistance to the air through which it passes.

Aerofoil   Small fins at the front of racing cars which help send the airflow away from the body.

CANAM   The CANadian AMerican Challenge, a top championship for specially made sports racing cars.

Circuits   Specially made courses or tracks for racing.

Cockpit   The small area where the race driver is seated.

Constructors Championship   The constructors, such as Williams, Ferrari etc., gain points in the Grand Prix races and this determines the team or car makers champion.

Formula 1   Motor racing's top category.

Fuel Injection   The means of exactly measuring the fuel flowing into the engine to obtain the best air/fuel mixture at slow, intermediate and very fast speeds.

Front Spoiler   See aerofoil.

Grand Prix   This is the top level in motor racing and is normally reserved for Formula 1 racing cars. The words are French and mean "big prize". Many other sports now use this term to indicate a major event.

Ground Effect   Lotus designed this way of using the air flowing beneath the car to increase road holding and therefore, top speed.

Impeller   The device that creates the air pressure to mix the air with the fuel in a turbocharger.

Lap Board   Or signal board. The board which pit crews use to advise their driver of information he may need, such as how many laps to go, or how far ahead of the next man he is. Most race teams also have radio links to the driver's helmet, but they continue to use this very early method.

Monocoque   The strong shell around the driver in a single-seater racing car which is beneath the bodywork and connects the car's chassis.

Pole Position   The favored place from which to start a motor race. It is called pole because in the first motor races the man who started actually used a flag at the end of a pole to signal the start. Practice runs determine who will start in pole position. These days most races are started using a system of red - get ready, green - go, lights.

Pit Crew   Each racing team has a permanent group of helpers to assist in the pits with tire changing, engine work, timekeeping and signals.

Racing Line   The fastest way to go through a bend, which drivers learn very quickly.

Radiator   A reservoir of water which passes through a system of pipes to help keep the engine from getting too hot. On turbo engines, there is also an inter-cooler which keeps the turbo from overheating.

Roll Bar   The strong safety hoop attached to the car chassis which helps protect the driver in case the car should flip upside down.

Sliding Skirt   Lotus introduced these "strips" to the bottom of the bodywork to help the car hug the track around corners.

Turbocharger   A means of increasing engine speed by using the wasted exhaust gases as energy to create the best possible air/fuel mixture.

USAC   United States senior championship for purpose-built racing cars.

Slipstream   In the same way that a car is aerodynamic to go through the air easily, if one car follows another closely and at high speed it can gain extra speed because the car in front is cutting through the air and doing most of the hard work for it.

Sponsorship   Businesses invest their money in teams, drivers, races and racetracks to be able to advertise their products which will be seen by millions of people.

Suspension   Racing cars have stiffer rides than road cars. The suspension smooths the ride by keeping the car at the same angle whatever the conditions helps increase cornering speed.

World Champion/Championship   Grand Prix racing has a number of events each year in which drivers and car makers score points. The driver and car maker with the most points is declared the champion.

Acknowledgements

We would like to thank and acknowledge the following people for the use of their photographs and transparencies.

p. 6/7   Orbis Publishing Ltd.
I.C.I. Fibres

p. 8/9   National Motor Museum

p. 10/11   National Motor Museum
B.B.C. Hulton Picture Library
I.C.I. Fibres
L.A.T. Photography

p.12/13   B.B.C. Hulton Picture Library
L.A.T. Photographic
Avenue Communications
Jeff Bloxham

p.14/15   I.C.I. Fibres
Blue Hawk Design Partnership

p. 16/17   L.A.T. Photographic
Colin Taylor Productions
Marlboro Motorsport Media Services
Orbis Publishing Ltd.

p. 18/19   Jardine P.R.
Marlborough Motorsport Media Services

p. 20/21   Orbis Publishing Ltd.
B.B.C. Hulton Picture Library
L.A.T. Photographic
Lotus Marketing Services Ltd.
Jardine P.R.

p. 22/23   L.A.T. Photographic
Porsche Cars (G.B.) Ltd.
Saab — Scania

p. 24/25   L.A.T. Photographic
Orbis Photographic Ltd.
Avenue Communications

p. 26/27   Orbis Publishing Ltd.
L.A.T. Photographic
Colin Taylor Productions

p. 28/29   National Motor Museum
L.A.T. Photographic
B.B.C. Hulton Picture Library

p. 30/31   Orbis Publishing
Marlborough Motorsport Media Services

Shell U.K. Oil

p. 32/33   Marlboro Motorsport Media Services

p. 34/35   L.A.T. Photographic
Marlboro Motorsport Media Services

p. 36/37   L.A.T. Photographic
I.C.I. Fibres

p. 38/39   B.B.C. Hulton Picture Library
Marlboro Motorsport Media Services
National Motor Museum

p. 40/41   I.C.I. Fibres

p. 42/43   I.C.I. Fibres
Canon (U.K.) Ltd.

p. 44/45   I.C.I. Fibres
Jardine P.R.

Cover Photographs:
Shell U.K. Oil
Orbis Publishing Ltd.

Frontispiece: Mobil

Illustrations by: Sharon Perks

Design and Production by: Susie Home

Written by: Paul Harmer

Index